NATIONAL
GEOGRAPHIC
KiDS

Funny FiLL-IN
MY GOLD MEDAL ADVENTURE

NATIONAL GEOGRAPHIC
WASHINGTON, D.C.

How to Play Funny Fill-In!

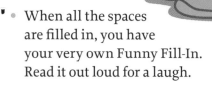

Love to create amazing stories? Good, because this one stars YOU. Get ready to laugh with all your friends—you can play with as many people as you want! Make sure to keep this book on your shelf. You'll want to read it again and again!

Are You Ready to Laugh?

- One person picks a story—you can start at the beginning, the middle, or the end of the book.

- Ask a friend to call out a word that the space asks for—noun, verb, or something else—and write it in the blank space. If there's more than one player, ask the next person to say a word. Extra points for creativity!

- When all the spaces are filled in, you have your very own Funny Fill-In. Read it out loud for a laugh.

- Want to play by yourself? Just fold over the page and use the cardboard insert at the back as a writing pad. Fill in the blank parts of speech list, and copy your answers into the story.

Fun Fact!

Make sure you check out the amazing **Fun Facts** that appear on every page!

Parts of Speech

To play the game, you'll need to know how to form sentences. This list with examples of the parts of speech and other terms will help you get started:

Noun: The name of a person, place, thing, or idea
Examples: tree, mouth, creature
*The **ocean** is full of colorful **fish**.*

Adjective: A word that describes a noun or pronoun
Examples: green, lazy, friendly
*My **silly** dog won't stop laughing!*

Verb: An action word. In the present tense, a verb often ends in –s or –ing. If the space asks for past tense, changing the vowel or adding a –d or –ed to the end usually will set the sentence in the past.
Examples: swim, hide, plays, running (present tense); biked, rode, jumped (past tense)
*The giraffe **skips** across the savanna.*
*The flower **opened** after the rain.*

Adverb: A word that describes a verb and usually ends in –ly
Examples: quickly, lazily, soundlessly
*Kelley **greedily** ate all the carrots.*

Plural: More than one
Examples: mice, telephones, wrenches
*Why are all the **doors** closing?*

Silly Word or Exclamation: A funny sound, a made-up word, a word you think is totally weird, or a noise someone or something might make
Examples: Ouch! No way! Foozleduzzle! Yikes!
*"**Darn!**" shouted Jim. "These cupcakes are sour!"*

Specific Words: There are many more ways to make your story hilarious. When asked for something like a number, animal, or body part, write in something you think is especially funny.

- your hometown
- silly word
- friend's name
- type of sport
- type of sport
- noun
- adjective ending in –est
- type of animal
- your age
- name of a song
- verb
- number
- dance move
- verb
- body part, plural
- body part, plural
- verb
- verb
- name of a country

MASCOT MANIA

Fun Fact! The first Olympic Games were held over 2,700 years ago to honor the Greek god Zeus.

Backflipping Fish

This year, _____ is hosting the World _____ Games. _____ and I are
(your hometown) (silly word) (friend's name)

auditioning to be the mascots. We play on _____ , _____ , and _____ teams,
(type of sport) (type of sport) (noun)

so we can't wait to see the amazing athletes at the games. The world's _____ athlete, Taylor
(adjective ending in –est)

_____ , will be there too, competing in _____ events. I'm dying to meet her and get
(type of animal) (your age)

a picture of us together! We hear "_____"—it's our cue! We _____ out in front of
(name of a song) (verb)

the judges, do _____ backflip(s), then _____ across the field. We _____ , then
(number) (dance move) (verb)

flip into the air and land with our _____ planted on the ground and our _____
(body part, plural) (body part, plural)

pointing at the judges. We break into our cheer: "Hey, judges, let's be bold! We're going to _____ !
(verb)

We're going to _____ ! We're going to go for the gold!" The judges go wild! We're
(verb)

the games' new mascots: the _____ Fish!
(name of a country)

SCORE
Flipper work __
Rhyming __
Swagger

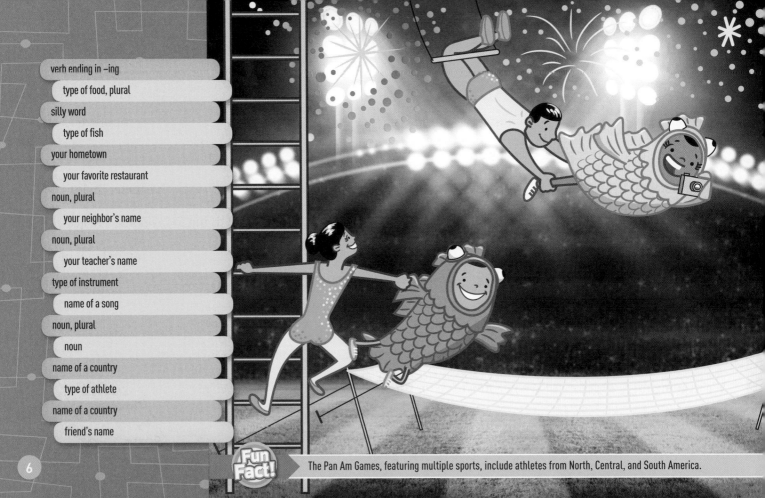

verb ending in –ing

type of food, plural

silly word

type of fish

your hometown

your favorite restaurant

noun, plural

your neighbor's name

noun, plural

your teacher's name

type of instrument

name of a song

noun, plural

noun

name of a country

type of athlete

name of a country

friend's name

6

The Pan Am Games, featuring multiple sports, include athletes from North, Central, and South America.

Hanging Around

After months of _____ and eating _____ , our training is over. Mr.
(verb ending in –ing)   (type of food, plural)   _____
                                                                                                              (silly word)

Zeus, one of the organizers, gives us _____ costumes to wear. We're ready for the games'
                                        (type of fish)

opening ceremonies! _____ has pulled out all the stops. _____ is
                       (your hometown)   (your favorite restaurant)

giving the athletes _____ as souvenirs. _____ is handing out coupons for
                      (noun, plural)   (your neighbor's name)

free _____ . _____ is playing a(n) _____ and belting out
       (noun, plural)   (your teacher's name)   (type of instrument)

"_____ ." There are fireworks in the shape of _____ ! Mr. Zeus sends us up
  (name of a song)   (noun, plural)

a ladder to do tricks with the acrobats. Before I know it, I'm swinging on a(n) _____ ! I'm about to catch
                                                                                  (noun)

my friend in midair when I see Taylor below me, carrying _____ 's flag. I whip out my
                                                          (name of a country)

camera—totally forgetting about my friend. Phew! A(n) _____ from _____
                                                        (type of athlete)   (name of a country)

catches _____ !
         (friend's name)

- noun
  - type of animal
- name of a country
  - friend's name
- verb ending in –s
  - something creepy
- name of a country
  - verb ending in –s
- verb
  - adjective
- something fuzzy
  - verb
- adjective
  - verb
- noun
  - same noun
- feeling
  - verb ending in –s
- adjective

8

Fun Fact! Brazil has won five World Cup soccer championships—more than any other country.

We're having a soccer match with all the mascots. Mr. Zeus blows his _____ *(noun)* and the game begins!

A(n) _____ *(type of animal)* from _____ *(name of a country)* has the ball, but _____ *(friend's name)* _____ *(verb ending in –s)* it and kicks it to me. A(n) _____ *(something creepy)* from _____ *(name of a country)* intercepts it and _____ *(verb ending in –s)* for our net. I _____ *(verb)* after it and get fouled by a(n) _____ *(adjective)* _____ *(something fuzzy)*. I get a free kick! I _____ *(verb)* at the ball, but my head is so _____ *(adjective)* that when I stop, I tip over and fall. Ack, the head's on backward! I can't see! I _____ *(verb)* around until I hit a(n) _____ *(noun)*. Wait, that was no _____ *(same noun)*. It was Taylor! She's not _____ *(feeling)*, though. She just fixes my head and laughingly says, "Did you take a dive?" Before I can answer, she _____ *(verb ending in –s)* onto the field. She's the star forward in the next game! She's so _____ *(adjective)*.

adverb ending in –ly

verb

something stinky

body part

verb

adjective

exclamation

body part

friend's name

verb

noun

noun

noun, plural

adjective ending in –er

adjective

type of animal

verb

verb

10

Fun Fact! Helen Skelton paddled 2,010 miles (3,235 km) of the Amazon River, winning the world record for longest kayak trip by a woman.

Shooting the Rapids

We're cheering on the kayakers as they _____ _____ through the rapids.

(adverb ending in –ly) (verb)

It sure is warm in this fish suit. I smell like a(n) _____. I decide to dip my _____

(something stinky) (body part)

in the water. I _____ over the edge, but my _____ fish head tips me into the water!

(verb) (adjective)

_____! I'm floating down the rapids in the _____ of the mascot suit! _____

(exclamation) (body part) (friend's name)

tries to _____ a(n) _____ to me and falls in, too. We're carried along by the river's

(verb) (noun)

_____ and finish first! We high-five the kayakers as they come in behind us. Mr. Zeus runs over

(noun)

and says, "The crowd loves you—it's time for a cheer!" So, we get out, looking like wet _____,

(noun, plural)

only _____, and break into our best dance move, the _____ _____.

(adjective ending in –er) (adjective) (type of animal)

"Hey, kayakers, let's be bold! We're going to _____! We're going to _____! We're going to

(verb) (verb)

go for the gold!"

adjective

   adjective ending in –er

verb

   something shiny, plural

your favorite athlete

   verb ending in –s

clothing item, plural

   something in your room

friend's name

   verb

type of fish

   boy's name

adjective ending in –est

   something round

verb ending in –s

   your country

verb ending in –s

   verb ending in –ed

large animal, plural

Fun Fact! Basketball was invented in 1891 by James Naismith, a Canadian phys ed teacher, while he was teaching in Massachusetts.

Nothing but Net

Our fish suits are all _____ , so Mr. Zeus gives us new ones. They're inflatable and so much
_____ *adjective ending in –er* ! We _____ *verb* over to the basketball event. Some of basketball's greatest
_____ *something shiny, plural* are playing. _____ *your favorite athlete* _____ *verb ending in –s* down the court,
wearing _____ *clothing item, plural* bigger than my _____ *something in your room* ! _____ *friend's name* and I
break into our cheer. The crowd joins us, and someone shouts, "I _____ *verb* you, _____ *type of fish* !" Just
then, _____ *boy's name* —the _____ *adjective ending in –est* guy on the team—chases the _____ *something round* to
the sidelines. He _____ *verb ending in –s* into me and bounces off! He flies through the air, slam-dunking the
ball on the way back down. I just helped _____ *your country* win the gold! The team _____ *verb ending in –s*
us. It's like being _____ *verb ending in –ed* by _____ *large animal, plural* . They're so big!

- verb ending in –ing
  - name of a nursery rhyme
- large number
  - verb
- verb
  - friend's name
- body part
  - adjective
- verb
  - something that floats, plural
- type of animal, plural
  - verb ending in –s
- noun
  - something that spins
- type of instrument
  - verb ending in –s
- noun, plural
  - type of bird, plural

14

Fun Fact! Synchronized swimmers aren't allowed to touch the bottom of the pool, even when they're lifting each other out of the water.

Schooled at the Pool

We're _____ at the synchronized swimming event. When _____
(verb ending in –ing)   (name of a nursery rhyme)

blares from the speakers, _____ women start dancing on the deck. They _____ into the
(large number)   (verb)

water and _____ together to the music. _____ lifts a(n) _____ into the air
(verb)   (friend's name)   (body part)

and smiles at the crowd. I do the same. We start copying the swimmers. We think we're _____,
(adjective)

but I'm not sure the swimmers agree. They pull us into the pool and _____ us around like
(verb)

_____ . Then they pretend to ride us like _____ ! Someone
(something that floats, plural)   (type of animal, plural)

_____ me into the air like I'm a(n) _____ and spins me like a(n) _____ .
(verb ending in –s)   (noun)   (something that spins)

One woman pretends to play me like a(n) _____ , while another _____ my
(type of instrument)   (verb ending in –s)

friend like a pair of _____ ! By the end, we're all laughing like _____ and
(noun, plural)   (type of bird, plural)

the crowd is cheering for more!

adjective ending in –est

noun

something pointy

type of animal

noun

number

body part

friend's name

something strong, plural

silly word

verb

something that floats

sound

fish body part

something soft, plural

Fun Fact! In 2010, 14-year-old Zak Crawford, from Corby, England, set a world record by sending an arrow flying 1,588.88 feet (484.29 m).

Bull's-Eye

Taylor is one of the _____ archers in the _____ event. We watch as she draws back
(adjective ending in –est) (noun)

her bow and lets the _____ fly. It's a(n) _____'s-eye! Mr. Zeus says, "That
(something pointy) (type of animal)

deserves a(n) _____!" It sure does! We sing our cheer, do _____ _____ flip(s),
(noun) (number) (body part)

and then _____ throws me into the air. A gust of _____ catches my suit.
(friend's name) (something strong, plural)

Oh no, I'm being blown onto the shooting range! There's an arrow heading straight for me! _____,
(silly word)

I've been hit! I _____ around like an untied _____, a(n) _____ sound
(verb) (something that floats) (sound)

following me. As I soar into the sky, I see Taylor looking up. I flap a(n) _____
(fish body part)

at her so she knows I'm okay. Suddenly the air in my suit runs out, and I crash-

land on a pile of _____. Phew!
(something soft, plural)

noun

your favorite band

verb

verb

verb

name of a country

name of a country

verb

adjective

verb

adjective

name of a relative

your favorite singer

noun

name of a song

friend's name

type of instrument

noun, plural

Fun Fact! Volleyball players jump about 300 times per match!

That night, Mr. Zeus covers the hole in my suit with a(n) _____ [noun] and tells us we can check out the concert. _____ [your favorite band] is playing, so we _____ [verb] right over. The crowd sees us and goes insane! They sing our cheer, "We're going to _____ [verb]! We're going to _____ [verb]! We're going to go for the gold!" Then they pick us up and suddenly we're crowd-surfing! At one point I get stuck between the volleyball teams from _____ [name of a country] and _____ [name of a country]. They seem to think I'm a giant fish-shaped volleyball! They _____ [verb] me back and forth until I'm so _____ [adjective] I want to _____ [verb]! Suddenly, a(n) _____ [adjective] woman who looks like _____ [name of a relative] spikes me. I bounce right back up! The crowd carries me to the stage, where _____ [your favorite singer] hands me the _____ [noun]. I belt out "_____ [name of a song]," then _____ [friend's name] does an amazing _____ [type of instrument] solo. We may never take these fish _____ [noun, plural] off!

verb

noun, plural

verb

verb

friend's name

body part

verb ending in –ing

body part

clothing item

type of food

feeling

verb

noun

same friend's name

verb ending in –s

verb

type of athlete, plural

verb

Judo, which means "the gentle way," first started in Japan about 130 years ago.

We walk into the judo event pretending to _____ like fish. The _____ in the stands start
                                              verb   noun, plural

cheering, "We _____ the fish! We _____ the fish!" Mr. Zeus says a pretend judo match might be
               verb   verb

fun, so I grab _____ by the _____ for a(n) _____ _____
                friend's name   body part   verb ending in –ing   body part

Throw. Instead, I'm pinned to the ground. Hey! I counter with a(n) _____ Drop, but I'm taken
                                                                    clothing item

down by a(n) _____ Bale Reversal! Ouch. Now I'm _____ . I _____ and try
              type of food   feeling   verb

a(n) _____ Storm. _____ bounces up, then _____ me again. I'm about to
      noun   same friend's name   verb ending in –s

try a Side _____ when I hear the crowd laughing. We're on the big screen, and in our inflatable suits,
            verb

we look like more like sumo _____ than judo masters. We _____ to each other and
                             type of athlete, plural   verb

the crowd. Then the real judokas throw us off the mats. They have some medals to win!

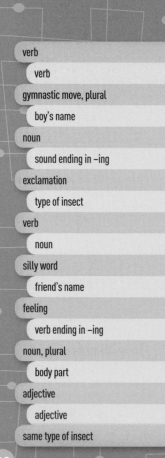

- verb
  - verb
- gymnastic move, plural
  - boy's name
- noun
  - sound ending in –ing
- exclamation
  - type of insect
- verb
  - noun
- silly word
  - friend's name
- feeling
  - verb ending in –ing
- noun, plural
  - body part
- adjective
  - adjective
- same type of insect

CATCH FISH FEVER!   GET IN THE SWIN

Fun Fact!

The only tennis players to win four Olympic gold medals—each—are sisters Venus and Serena Williams.

No Love

"Hey, tennis players, let's be bold! We're going to _____ ! We're going to _____ ! We're going to
                                                    verb   verb

go for the gold!" we cheer, then do _____ . The crowd roars its approval, then hushes. Tennis
                                        gymnastic move, plural

star _____ Fedor is about to serve. It's so quiet, you could hear a(n) _____ drop. Wait,
         boy's name   noun

what's that _____ sound? _____ ! A(n) _____ is in my suit! I _____
              sound ending in –ing   exclamation   type of insect   verb

loudly and try to get away from it—not easy since it's trapped in here. Oh no, I've run onto the court! Fedor

misses the _____ and shouts, "You _____ ! Get off of here!" _____ and Mr. Zeus
              noun   silly word   friend's name

chase me around, trying to help. Ouch! Fedor's so _____ , he's _____ _____
                                                      feeling   verb ending in –ing   noun, plural

at us! One bounces off my suit and hits Fedor in the _____ . Now he's really
                                                        body part

_____ ! The _____ _____ , Mr. Zeus, and my
   adjective   adjective   same type of insect

friend and I all run for it!

23

verb

   verb

verb

   type of fish

verb ending in –s

   large number

noun, plural

   adjective ending in –er

something you ride

   type of animal

friend's name

   verb ending in –s

adjective

   something that flies

something slimy, plural

   adjective

24

Fun Fact! The height of a horse is measured in "hands." One hand is equal to four inches (10 cm).

Horse Play

The equestrian events are under way. I love horses, but they don't love me in my fish suit. Mr. Zeus says

I could _____ one, but it won't _____ for me. Then I see my friend trying to _____ one.
        verb   verb   verb

When the horse sees a(n) _____ on its back, it _____ off! It jumps _____
                         type of fish   verb ending in −s   large number

_____ , while my friend hangs on for dear life! Suddenly, _____ than a
noun, plural   adjective ending in −er

speeding _____ , a woman on a(n) _____ races past me. It's Taylor! She's
         something you ride   type of animal

chasing _____ on the runaway! Taylor _____ and the _____ horse
        friend's name   verb ending in −s   adjective

stops. My friend flies through the air like a(n) _____ , landing in a puddle of
                                                 something that flies

_____ . Taylor leaps down and helps my friend up. Then, before I can get there,
something slimy, plural

Taylor jumps onto her horse and rides off into the sunset like a(n) _____ cowboy.
                                                                    adjective

25

adjective

   noun, plural

adjective

   something fluffy

famous male athlete

   famous female athlete

clothing item

   type of athlete

name of a country

   adjective

something spicy

   type of athlete

name of a country

   something sticky

color

   famous swimmer

adjective

   type of bird

26

Fun Fact! The five Olympic rings represent the Americas, Asia, Africa, Australia, and Europe.

This mascot business makes us _____ (adjective)! We decide to check out the food in

the athletes' cafeteria. Usually only _____ (noun, plural) are allowed in, but the guards see

us and break out into some of our signature moves, like the _____ (adjective) _____ (something fluffy).

They're fans! The athletes seem excited to see us, too. _____ (famous male athlete) begs us to sit with him.

_____ (famous female athlete) comes over and asks us to sign her _____ (clothing item). They know we're just

kids in fish suits, right? Then they all start bringing us their favorite foods. A(n) _____ (type of athlete) from

_____ (name of a country) brings us _____ (adjective) _____ (something spicy). A(n) _____ (type of athlete)

from _____ (name of a country) brings us _____ (something sticky) in a(n) _____ (color) sauce. Then they

all sing our cheer and start dancing. _____ (famous swimmer) kind of moves like a(n) _____ (adjective)

_____ (type of bird)! This is crazy. It's like we're famous!

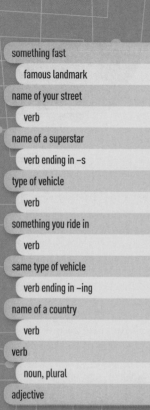

- something fast
  - famous landmark
- name of your street
  - verb
- name of a superstar
  - verb ending in –s
- type of vehicle
  - verb
- something you ride in
  - verb
- same type of vehicle
  - verb ending in –ing
- name of a country
  - verb
- verb
  - noun, plural
- adjective

MARATHON FINISH LINE

NEED TO CHEAT? CALL US!

CH ★ 888

Fun Fact! In 1904, an American marathon runner finished first by getting a ride in a car. When he was caught, he said it had been a joke!

The marathon has begun and Taylor's running like a(n) _____ *something fast* ! She's just past the

_____ *famous landmark* on _____ *name of your street* and is in the lead. We see another runner

_____ *verb* by. She looks like _____ *name of a superstar* . She also looks sick. She _____ *verb ending in –s*

down an alley. I follow to see if she's okay and see her get in a(n) _____ *type of vehicle* . I _____ *verb* for

a(n) _____ *something you ride in* and tell the driver to _____ *verb* after her. When the runner's _____ *same type of vehicle*

stops, I film her getting out and _____ *verb ending in –ing* back onto the course. She crosses the finish line

and wins! Her anthem begins: "_____ *name of a country* , we _____ *verb* you, and will _____ *verb* to

protect your _____ *noun, plural* ." I show the judges the video, and they snatch back

the medal and give it to Taylor. I want to congratulate her, but we're

late for the _____ *adjective* event!

noun, plural

    color

adjective

    verb

noun

    verb

verb

    name of a cartoon character

verb

    noun

something bouncy

    friend's name

mythical animal

    verb

noun, plural

    adjective

noun

    body part

large number

In ancient times, gymnasts vaulted over live bulls!

We're cheering on the gymnasts. Taylor's taken gold in the uneven _____ (noun, plural) and a(n) _____ (color) for the _____ (adjective) beam. I try to _____ (verb) with her as she leaves the athlete's _____ (noun) , but Mr. Zeus wants us to perform on the trampolines. I _____ (verb) on, ready to lay down my _____ (verb) Jump, followed by a Half-_____ (name of a cartoon character) . Instead, I _____ (verb) into the ceiling, rebound off a(n) _____ (noun) , then hit the _____ (something bouncy) . I fly toward _____ (friend's name) , who was attempting a(n) _____ (mythical animal) Turn, and we _____ (verb) off each other. We're flying around like _____ (noun, plural) in a pinball machine! Finally, we get used to the extra bounce, and it's _____ (adjective) !

When we nail the first ever tandem Full _____ (noun) , people stop screaming and cheer us on. My friend does a Three-Quarter _____ (body part) Roll off my belly. And, for the finale, we act like fish out of water, performing a record _____ (large number) flips and pikes. The crowd goes wild!

adjective

    noun

verb ending in –s

    friend's name

body part, plural

    verb

verb

    noun

adjective

    type of bird

verb ending in –ing

    body part, plural

noun

    something wet, plural

sound

    type of sport

feeling

    type of sports equipment

32

Fun Fact! The current record for pole vaulting is 20 feet 2.5 inches (6.16 m), set by Renaud Lavillenie from France.

The pole-vaulters are _____ , so Mr. Zeus asks us to entertain everyone. My friend grabs

adjective

a(n) _____ , runs, and _____ . The bar falls and _____ , _____

noun verb ending in –s friend's name body part, plural

flailing, lands in the pit. The audience laughs and cheers, "Hey, Fish, let's be bold! We're going to _____ !

verb

We're going to _____ ! We're going to go for the gold!" I wave at them, grab a(n) _____ , run,

verb noun

and leap. I love the feeling of flying through the air! Wait, what's that? It's an _____ bald

adjective

_____ and it's _____ straight for me! It must think I'm a real fish! It digs

type of bird verb ending in –ing

its _____ into me and now I have another _____ in my suit! The

body part, plural noun

bird carries me across the sky, then drops me in some _____ with

something wet, plural

a(n) _____ . It's a(n) _____ pool! The players are _____ to

sound type of sport feeling

see me. They pass me a(n) _____ and ask me to join in!

type of sports equipment

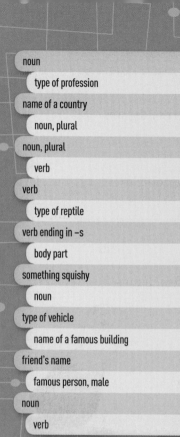

- noun
  - type of profession
- name of a country
  - noun, plural
- noun, plural
  - verb
- verb
  - type of reptile
- verb ending in –s
  - body part
- something squishy
  - noun
- type of vehicle
  - name of a famous building
- friend's name
  - famous person, male
- noun
  - verb

34

Fun Fact! If athletes go over the foul line in the long jump, modeling clay is used to show their footprint.

Model Mix-Up

We want to watch track and _____ (noun) events, but the _____ (type of profession) of _____ (name of a country) is making a speech about _____ (noun, plural) and national _____ (noun, plural). Boring! We _____ (verb) a board lying near us. Hey, there's some modeling clay on it! I _____ (verb) a bunch and make a(n) _____ (type of reptile). My friend _____ (verb ending in –s) some with his _____ (body part) and makes a(n) _____ (something squishy). We start to see who can make the best shapes. My _____ (noun) sculpture is pretty awesome, but his _____ (type of vehicle) model is good, too. Then we see some sand! I build _____ (name of a famous building) and _____ (friend's name) makes _____ (famous person, male). It looks just like him! Suddenly, some guy lands on my sand _____ (noun). It's ruined! I'm about to _____ (verb) at him when I see a judge run over to our modeling clay sculptures. Is she judging them? Oops! It turns out the modeling clay and sand were for the long jump. Luckily that was just the practice jump!

- your name
  - body part
- number
  - exclamation
- your name
  - name of a country
- adjective
  - verb ending in –ing
- noun
  - verb
- verb ending in –s
  - something light
- verb ending in –ing
  - noun
- verb
  - adjective
- noun

Fun Fact! Swimmer Michael Phelps eats 12,000 calories a day. That's the equivalent of 114 bananas!

Diving In

Famed diver _____ (your name) soars off the platform in a(n) _____ (body part) dive,

does _____ (number) somersault(s), and slices into the pool. _____ (exclamation)! _____ (your name) has won the

gold for _____ (name of a country)! As the medal ceremony begins, I look over and notice a(n) _____ (adjective)

little kid _____ (verb ending in –ing) up to the _____ (noun) high above. Oh no! No one seems to notice!

I _____ (verb) after her, but before I get there, she _____ (verb ending in –s) off the platform! I dive into the

water to save her, but the _____ (something light) in my suit pulls me right back to the surface. I yank a patch

off one of the holes in my suit, and suddenly I'm _____ (verb ending in –ing) through the water toward her like

a(n) _____ (noun)! I grab her as I _____ (verb) past and place her safely on the deck. Everyone's cheering!

I'm a hero! As my reward, the kid gives me a big, _____ (adjective) _____ (noun). Aw.

- adjective
  - noun
- type of celebration
  - noun
- verb
  - noun, plural
- verb
  - noun, plural
- verb
  - noun
- adjective
  - verb
- noun
  - friend's name
- body part
  - verb
- something that floats, plural
  - name of a holiday

HOPSCOTCH CHAMPIONS

12th ANNUAL CARTWHEEL CHAMPIONS

JACKS CH

Fun Fact! Since the modern Olympics began in 1896, the United States has won 2,400 medals—more than any other country!

Beached Balls

Mr. Zeus asks us to do a(n) _____ routine with the gymnasts before their rhythmic _____ starts.
adjective   noun

He adds helium to our suits, saying it will be fun! We practically float into the gym like _____
                                                                                    type of celebration

balloons. We pirouette across the _____ , then _____ up, swirling long _____
                                  noun   verb   noun, plural

through the air. I _____ through _____ , but instead of landing, I float off into the crowd!
                   verb   noun, plural

They _____ me around like a giant beach _____ until I'm _____ . When they throw
     verb   noun   adjective

me back, I'm just in time for my friend to _____ over me and shoot off into the stands, too!
                                           verb

I grab a long _____ and throw one end to _____ , who catches it with
              noun   friend's name

his/her _____ . I _____ it through the air, and my friend holds on and
        body part   verb

pretends to be a fish on a line. As the crowd cheers, the gymnasts pull us out of the

gym like _____ in a(n) _____ parade!
         something that floats, plural   name of a holiday

39

- adverb ending in –ly
- verb ending in –s
- verb ending in –s
- adjective
- type of animal
- noun
- noun, plural
- something gross
- friend's name
- noun
- large number
- verb ending in –s
- body part
- clothing item
- same body part
- verb ending in –ing
- verb
- body part, plural
- something stinky

FINISH LINE

Fun Fact!

The pentathlon involves five sports: fencing, shooting, swimming, riding, and running.

Taylor rocks at the pentathlon. During the fencing, she _____ _____
a hit every time. In the pool, she _____ her way to another win. At the show-jumping course,

(adverb ending in –ly) *(verb ending in –s)*

(verb ending in –s)

she's given a(n) _____ _____ . Together they leap over a brick _____ and

(adjective) *(type of animal)* *(noun)*

some _____ . Another win! We start our cheer, but I slip in _____ , and

(noun, plural) *(something gross)*

_____ has to hose me down. When the race starts, Taylor's in the lead. She reaches the

(friend's name)

shooting range, fires her laser _____ , and makes all _____ shots. On her fourth lap,

(noun) *(large number)*

she _____ and twists her _____ . Is this the end? No! She ties her _____

(verb ending in –s) *(body part)* *(clothing item)*

around her _____ , then she's up and _____ . She wins! I run to congratulate

(same body part) *(verb ending in –ing)*

her, but as I _____ , people hold their _____ . I still smell like horse _____ !

(verb) *(body part, plural)* *(something stinky)*

I can't meet Taylor like this!

name of your school

verb

verb ending in –ed

adjective

type of fish

type of animal, plural

adjective

clothing item

color

something slimy, plural

body part, plural

number

friend's name

silly word

noun

something wet

verb

noun

noun

GO FISH

WE ❤ FISH

WE ❤ FISH

5

GROUPER GROUPIE

Fun Fact! The steeplechase gets its name from Ireland, where horses would race over obstacles between two churches.

We're at _____ to cheer on the races. The athletes line up for the steeplechase. We call, "Hey,
            name of your school

runners, let's be bold! We're going to _____ ! We're going to—Ow!" Someone just _____
                                         verb   *verb ending in –ed*

a(n) _____ fish at me! A kid screams, "I love you, _____ !" Then people swarm us like a pack
       adjective   *type of fish*

of _____ . "Can I have your autograph?" asks a woman in a(n) _____ _____
    type of animal, plural   *adjective*   *clothing item*

with a(n) _____ fish pattern. "Do you eat _____ ?" asks a kid wearing fake
            color   *something slimy, plural*

_____ . "Loan me _____ dollar(s)?" says someone else. We're surrounded!
body part, plural   *number*

_____ takes off toward the _____ -athlon. I hit the steeplechase
   friend's name   *silly word*

course! I jump a(n) _____ and land in _____ . I keep running, but the
                      noun   *something wet*

suit's too heavy! I tear it off and hide among the runners as we _____ toward
                                                                    verb

a(n) _____ . The race ends, but I keep going! Even the athletes want my _____ !
       noun   *noun*

43

- your age
- your country
- adjective
- sound
- body part, plural
- verb
- friend's name
- verb
- adverb ending in –ly
- name of a country
- name of a country
- verb ending in –s
- same friend
- verb
- type of animal, plural
- adjective
- noun

Fun Fact! In one of the races in the ancient Olympics, athletes wore helmets, shields, greaves (shin armor), and not a stitch of clothing!

Going for Gold

The best thing just happened! _____ of _____'s runners have come down with a
                                      your age   your country

cold. Okay, so not the best thing for them. But, after seeing us run away from our _____ fans, the
                                                                                        adjective

games' committee says we can race for our nation! No one recognizes us without our suits on. One runner

says, "My mom came to see the Fish cheer. Where are they?" Sorry, we have a race to win! There's

a(n) _____ , and we're off! _____ pumping, we _____ to the front of the
        sound   body part, plural   verb

pack. _____ and I _____ as _____ as we can. We pull ahead of the
        friend's name   verb   adverb ending in –ly

runner from _____ , and then it's just us. The finish line's in sight! Suddenly, a runner
                  name of a country

from _____ _____ into my friend. I pull _____ up and
        name of a country   verb ending in –s   same friend

we _____ like _____ to catch up. But it's too late. We tie for fourth. It's better
      verb   type of animal, plural

than last! We celebrate with our favorite dance, the _____ _____ !
                                                          adjective   noun

large number

adjective

verb ending in –ing

adjective

friend's name

adjective

verb

verb

something you ride

feeling

adjective

name of a season

noun, plural

adjective

verb ending in –s

noun

type of sport

exclamation

Fun Fact! During the 16 days of the Summer Olympics, more than 10,000 athletes compete in 302 events in 26 sports.

The closing ceremonies have begun. Taylor won _____ gold medals and is even more
_____ (large number)
(adjective) . I'll never meet her now! I watch her _____ on the _____
(verb ending in –ing) (adjective)

screen. Then I see _____ and me up on the screen. The crowd goes insane. There's a video
(friend's name)

of all our _____ feats and fails! I _____ when I see us trying to _____
(adjective) (verb) (verb)

_____ in fish suits! I'm _____ , but Mr. Zeus calls us to the stage. He says, "You
(something you ride) (feeling)

were _____ mascots! Will you come to the _____ games?" It turns out everyone
(adjective) (name of a season)

has been glued to their _____ to see what we'd do next—we broke the Internet! We're
(noun, plural)

international _____ stars! Taylor _____ up and asks if she can get a picture
(adjective) (verb ending in –s)

with us. Then she gives us each a(n) gold _____ for being such great sports and asks us if we'd like
(noun)

to go play _____ with her. _____ !
(type of sport) (exclamation)

Callie Broaddus, *Art Director;* **Jennifer MacKinnon,** *Writer;* **Dan Sipple,** *Illustrator*
Editorial, Design, and Production by Plan B Book Packagers

Credits

Cover: Katalinks/Shutterstock; **4** Arnonpix/Shutterstock; **6** Krivosheev Vitaly/Shutterstock; **8** Nexus7/Shutterstock; **10** Lerka 555/Shutterstock; **12** Prophoto 14/Shutterstock; **14** Glow On Concept/Shutterstock; **16** Mirrorimage-NL/Shutterstock; **18** Hurry/Shutterstock; **20** Lilyana Vynogradova/Shutterstock; **22** Leonard Zhukovsky/Shutterstock; **24** Callie Broaddus; **26** Hxdbzxy/Shutterstock; **28** Pisa Photography/Shutterstock; **30** Thomas Coex/Getty Images; **32** Zodebala/Shutterstock; **34** Ball LunLa/Shutterstock; **36** Trek and Shoot/iStockphoto; **38** Paparazzo Family/Shutterstock; **40** Anastasios 71/Shutterstock; **42** Ivica Drusany/Shutterstock; **44** Dotshock/Shutterstock; **46** Regien Paassen/Shutterstock

Since 1888, the National Geographic Society has funded more than 12,000 research, exploration, and preservation projects around the world. The Society receives funds from National Geographic Partners LLC, funded in part by your purchase. A portion of the proceeds from this book supports this vital work.

For more information, please visit nationalgeographic.com, call 1-800-647-5463, or write to the following address:

National Geographic Partners, LLC, 1145 17th Street N.W. Washington, D.C. 20036-4688 U.S.A.

Visit us online at nationalgeographic.com/books

For librarians and teachers: ngchildrensbooks.org

More for kids from National Geographic: kids.nationalgeographic.com

For information about special discounts for bulk purchases, please contact National Geographic Books Special Sales: ngspecsales@ngs.org

For rights or permissions inquiries, please contact National Geographic Books Subsidiary Rights: ngbookrights@ngs.org

ISBN: 978-1-4263-2404-8

Printed in China
16/RRDS/1